PLANETS

MERCURY

Alexis Roumanis

D0126151

Go to **www.av2books.com**, and enter this book's unique code.

BOOK CODE

E 2 3 6 3 6 3

AV²by Weigl brings you media enhanced books that support active learning.

AV² provides enriched content that supplements and complements this book. Weigl's AV² books strive to create inspired learning and engage young minds in a total learning experience.

Your AV² Media Enhanced books come alive with...

Audio
Listen to sections of the book read aloud.

Video
Watch informative video clips.

Embedded Weblinks
Gain additional information for research.

Try This!
Complete activities and hands-on experiments.

Key Words
Study vocabulary, and complete a matching word activity.

Quizzes
Test your knowledge.

Slide Show
View images and captions, and prepare a presentation.

... and much, much more!

Published by AV² by Weigl
350 5th Avenue, 59th Floor New York, NY 10118
Websites: www.av2books.com   www.weigl.com

Library of Congress Cataloging-in-Publication Data

Roumanis, Alexis, author.
 Mercury / Alexis Roumanis.
    pages cm. -- (Planets)
 Includes index.
 ISBN 978-1-4896-3292-0 (hard cover : alk. paper) -- ISBN 978-1-4896-3293-7 (soft cover : alk. paper)
-- ISBN 978-1-4896-3294-4 (single user ebook) -- ISBN 978-1-4896-3295-1 (multi-user ebook)
 1. Mercury (Planet)--Juvenile literature. I. Title.
 QB611.R68 2016
 523.41--dc23
                                     2014041519

Printed in the United States of America in Brainerd, Minnesota
1 2 3 4 5 6 7 8 9 0   19 18 17 16 15

022015
WEP081214

Project Coordinator: Katie Gillespie Art Director: Terry Paulhus

Weigl acknowledges Getty Images and iStock as the primary image suppliers for this title.

MERCURY

CONTENTS

What Is Mercury?

Mercury is a planet. It moves in a path around the Sun. Mercury is the closest planet to the Sun.

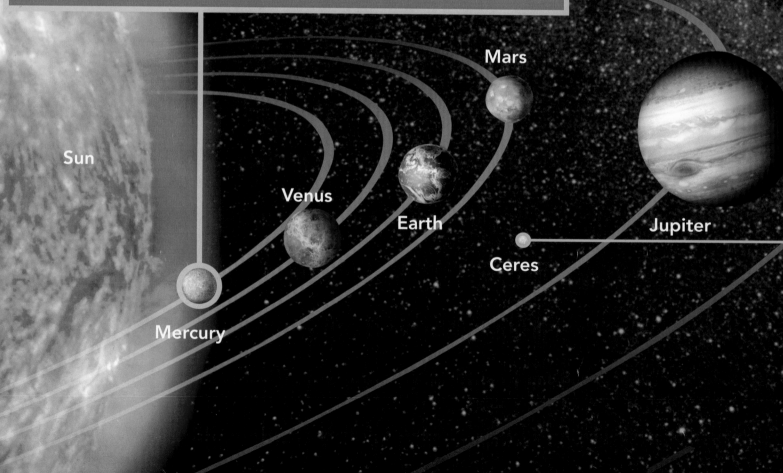

Sun

Mercury

Venus

Earth

Mars

Ceres

Jupiter

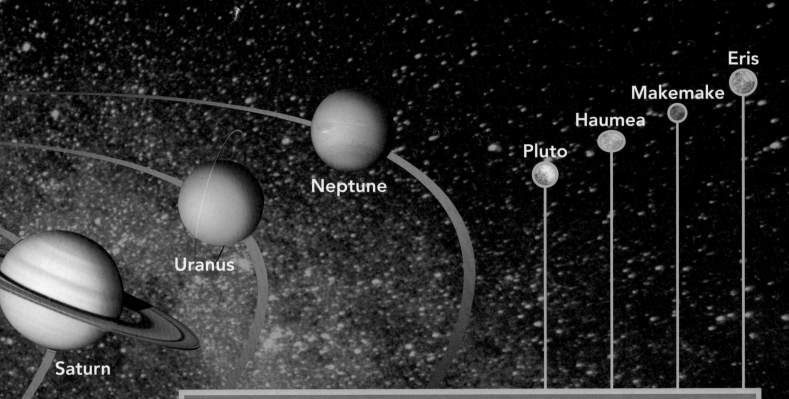

Saturn

Uranus

Neptune

Pluto

Haumea

Makemake

Eris

Dwarf Planets

Dwarf planets are round objects that move around the Sun. Unlike planets, they share their part of space with other objects.

How Big Is Mercury?

Mercury is the smallest planet in the solar system. It is about one third as wide as Earth.

Earth

Mercury

What Is Mercury Made Of?

Mercury is a rocky planet. It is mostly made of iron. This makes Mercury very heavy.

9

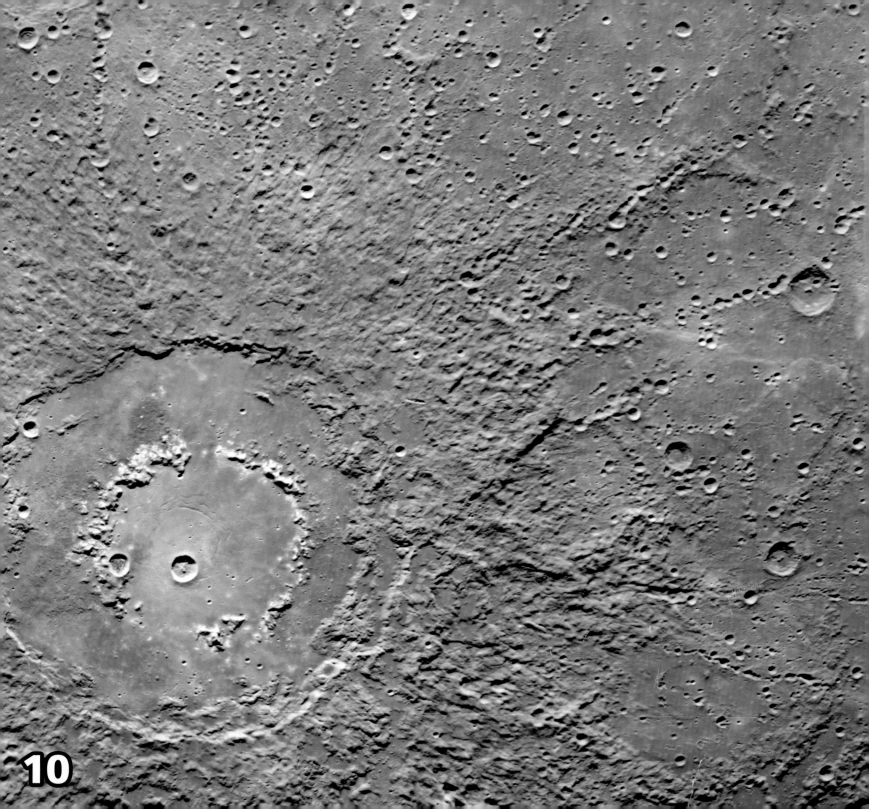

10

What Does Mercury Look Like?

Mercury looks like Earth's moon. Mercury's surface is covered in holes called craters. Some of these craters were made by meteorites hitting the planet.

What Is the Caloris Basin?

The Caloris Basin is a large crater on Mercury's surface. It is about one third as long as the United States. The Caloris Basin was made billions of years ago.

Venus

Mercury

Mercury's Missing Moon

Mercury has no moon. Venus is the only other planet without a moon. Mercury may once have been Venus's moon.

Who First Studied Mercury?

The first person to study Mercury was called Giovanni. He watched the planet through a telescope.

17

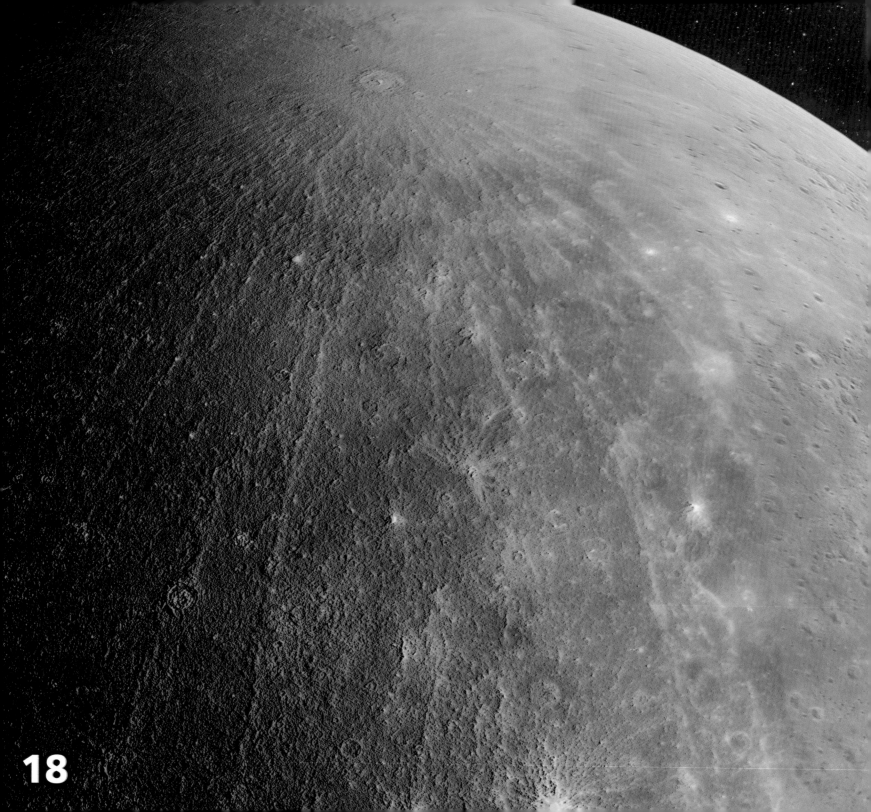

18

How Is Mercury Different from Earth?

Each planet is a different temperature. Mercury is much hotter than Earth. It is one of the hottest planets in the solar system.

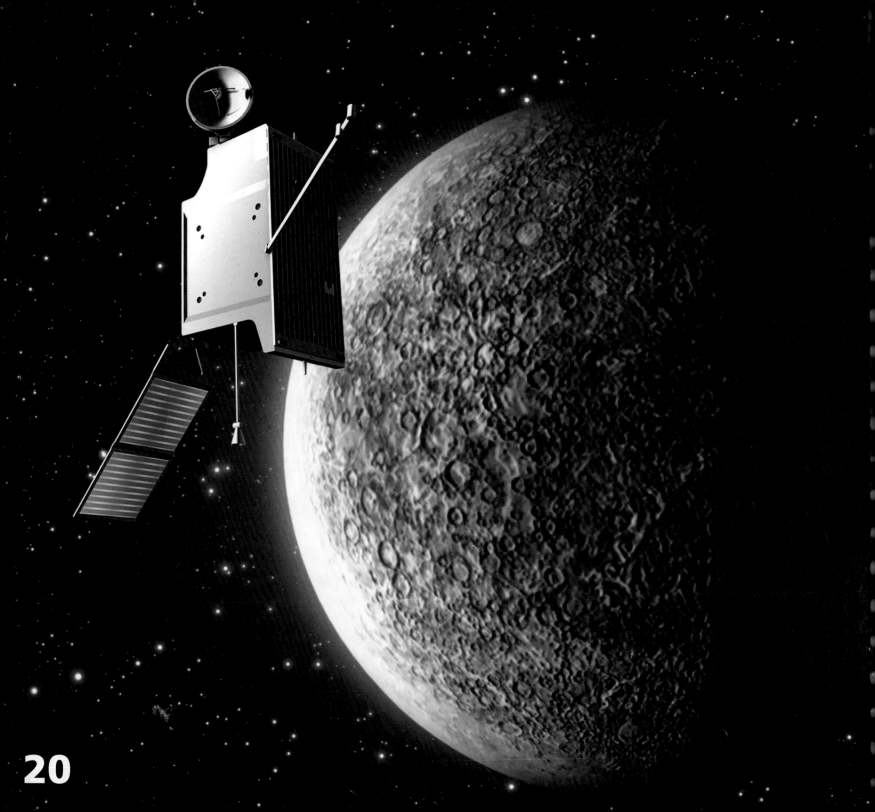

How Do We Learn about Mercury Today?

Scientists send vehicles called probes into space to study the solar system. A space probe called *BepiColombo* will launch in 2016. It will take almost eight years to reach Mercury.

MERCURY FACTS

This page provides more detail about the interesting facts found in the book. They are intended to be used by adults as a learning support to help young readers round out their knowledge of each planet featured in the *Planets* series.

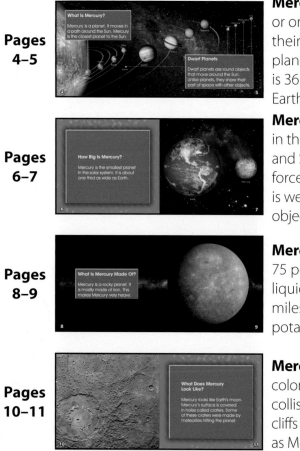

Pages 4–5

Mercury is a planet. Planets are round objects that move around, or orbit, a star, with enough mass to clear smaller objects from their orbit. Earth's solar system has eight planets, five known dwarf planets, and many other space objects that all orbit the Sun. Mercury is 36 million miles (58 million kilometers) from the Sun. It takes 88 Earth days for Mercury to make one orbit around the Sun.

Pages 6–7

Mercury is the smallest planet in the solar system. Two moons in the solar system are larger than Mercury. Jupiter's moon, Ganymede, and Saturn's moon, Titan, are both larger than the planet. Gravity is a force that pulls objects toward a planet's center. The force of gravity is weaker on Mercury than it is on Earth. A 100-pound (45-kilogram) object on Earth would only weigh 38 pounds (17 kg) on Mercury.

Pages 8–9

Mercury is a rocky planet. Mercury's center, or core, makes up 75 percent of the planet. This core is made up of partly molten, or liquid, iron. Mercury's outer shell is called the crust. It is about 250 miles (400 km) thick. The planet is made up of a large amount of potassium and sulfur.

Pages 10–11

Mercury looks like Earth's moon. From space, Mercury is gray in color with many impact craters. Mercury's craters were shaped by collisions with asteroids, comets, and meteorites. There are also large cliffs that reach up to 1 mile (1.6 km) in height. These cliffs were formed as Mercury's interior cooled and contracted over time.

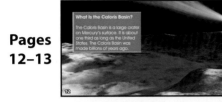

The Caloris Basin is a large crater on Mercury's surface. It was discovered by the space probe, *Mariner 10,* in 1974. The Caloris Basin spans about 960 miles (1,550 km) in diameter. It is one of the largest impact basins in the solar system. Experts believe that the force of the impact created a ring of mountains about 2 miles (3 km) high that surrounds the crater.

Mercury has no moon. Some scientists believe that Mercury was once Venus's moon, but it broke away from Venus's orbit. This may explain why neither planet has a moon. Also, it could have been difficult for Mercury's weak gravitational pull to attract a moon.

The first person to study Mercury was called Giovanni. Many ancient civilizations observed the planet. The early Greeks thought Mercury was two different objects, which they named Apollo and Hermes. However, it was not until Giovanni Schiaparelli began to study Mercury in the 1800s that a detailed map of the planet was created. A ridge on Mercury was named after Schiaparelli in 1976.

Each planet is a different temperature. The average temperature on Mercury is 332° Fahrenheit (167° Celsius). On Earth, the average temperature is 46° F (8° C). The only planet hotter than Mercury is Venus. An atmosphere is made of gases that surround a planet. Since Mercury is so close to the Sun, it has no atmosphere. Venus has a thick atmosphere, which helps keep in the heat.

Scientists send vehicles called probes into space to study the solar system. *BepiColombo* is a joint effort between the European Space Agency and the Japan Aerospace Exploration Agency. It will launch in July 2016 and arrive in orbit around Mercury in January 2024. Among other objectives, *BepiColombo* will study the structure, composition, and origins of Mercury.

KEY WORDS

Research has shown that as much as 65 percent of all written material published in English is made up of 300 words. These 300 words cannot be taught using pictures or learned by sounding them out. They must be recognized by sight. This book contains 65 common sight words to help young readers improve their reading fluency and comprehension. This book also teaches young readers several important content words. These words are paired with pictures to aid in learning and improve understanding.

Page	Sight Words First Appearance	Page	Content Words First Appearance
4	a, around, in, is, it, moves, the, to, what	4	Mercury, path, planet, Sun
5	are, of, other, part, that, their, they, with	5	dwarf planets, objects, space
6	about, as, big, Earth, how, one	6	solar system
8	made, makes, this, very	8	iron
11	by, does, like, look, some, these, were	11	craters, holes, meteorites, moon, surface
12	large, long, on, States, was, years	12	Caloris Basin, United States
15	been, has, have, may, no, once, only, without	15	Venus
16	first, he, study, through, who	16	Giovanni, person, telescope
19	different, each, from, much, than	19	temperature
21	almost, do, into, learn, take, we, will	21	*BepiColombo*, probes, scientists, vehicles